Hello, my name is **A**lex. I am a dinosaur.

My **B**est friend is Riley.
We both enjoy **C**hasing rabbits and squirrels. But not porcupines!

One Day we saw a boy named Joseph telling his eleven brothers about his dreams. The brothers were mad. They were full of Envy over his coat of many colors that he received from his father, Jacob.

Riley and I were throwing a **F**ootball while we watched Joseph and his brothers arguing about his dreams. But **G**od was watching over Joseph.

One day Jacob asked Joseph to go check on **H**is brothers
who were watching their father's flock.

Riley and **I** watched as his brothers threw Joseph into a well.
The brothers left **J**oseph in the pit and sat down to eat a meal together
For once we did not feel like eating anything—even chocolate dipped
bananas. Thinking about Joseph in that pit made us sad.

Joseph's brother's decided to sell Joseph as a slave.
These new men took Joseph down to Egypt. Riley and I looked
for a Key to free Joseph—but we could not find one.

Riley and I packed our bags and decided to follow Joseph
down to Egypt. Along the way Riley mistook our GPS for a video game.
The game was fun, but we got Lost!

Once we **M**ade it down to Egypt, we found out Joseph had been
sold to a man named Potiphar. Potiphar? Riley laughed at that name.
She kept asking "What is a pot for?" I just shook my head.

After we had gotten settled in, we snuck down to Potiphar's house
to see how Joseph was doing. We looked through a window
and saw him running away from Potiphar's wife. Joseph knew God did
Not want him being with the Potiphar's wife.

Riley **O**verheard Potiphar's wife make false charges against Joseph.

We watched as Joseph was thrown into **P**rison.
We had to keep **Q**uiet so we would not get in trouble.

Riley and I were able to sneak past the guards and get a good look at Joseph in his cell! He didn't look **S**ad or worried. Even sitting in prison Joseph did not give up his faith in God.

One day Joseph met a Baker and Butler in prison
who had very Troubling dreams.

Joseph told the Butler and Baker that with God's help,
he could **U**nderstand the meaning of their dreams.

For the butler, the dream meant good,
but for the baker it meant Very bad.

After three days, **W**hat Joseph said about their dreams came true.

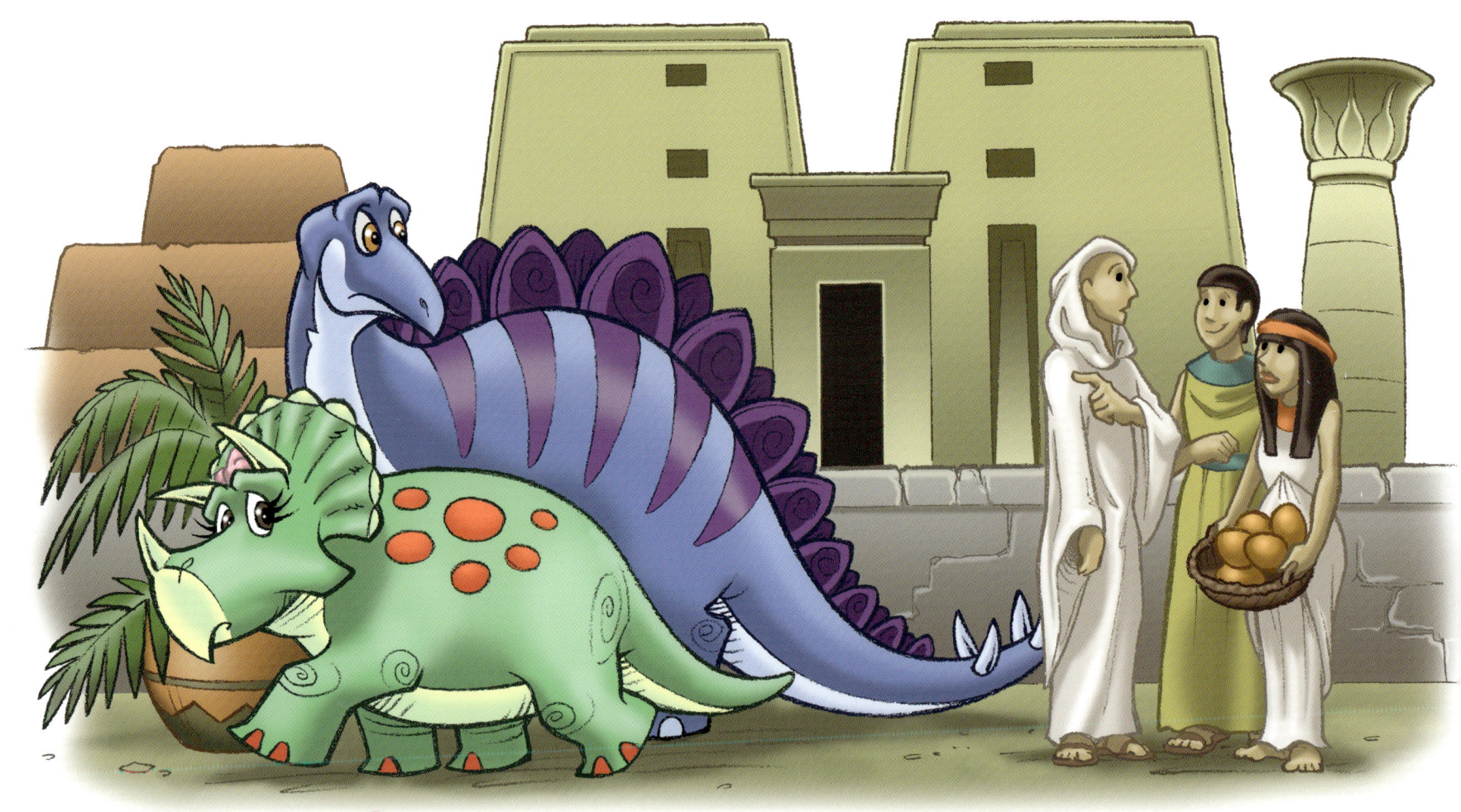

Two years later, as we were walking around Egypt,
we heard Pharaoh had also had e**X**tremely strange
dreams about seven fat cows and seven skinny cows.
We knew Joseph could help interpret his dreams.

We snuck into the palace as the butler was telling Pharaoh about Joseph, who had interpreted his dreams while he was in prison. You could have heard a pin drop until Riley knocked over a big Zebra statue.

Joseph was brought to the Pharoah who asked him to interpret his dreams. We listened in shock as Joseph told Pharaoh that God was sending seven years of much food, followed by seven years of no food. Suddenly we found our stomachs rumbling at the thought of no food. Riley's eyes got really big at the thought of not being able to eat ice cream for seven years

Then Joseph suggested for Pharaoh to select a wise man to save food. So during the seven years of plenty they could store food for the seven years of famine. Pharaoh declared that Joseph should be the man for that job. Riley started crying tears of happiness. I almost did, but I quickly wiped them away.

Joseph's interpretation came true again. Riley and I loved those seven years of plentiful food. But those were followed by seven years of famine Pharaoh put Joseph in charge of saving food for the famine. Riley and I managed to save some extra chocolate covered bananas and ice cream.

Eventually, Joseph's brothers came looking for food and were reunited with Joseph. Joseph invited his whole family to come down to Egypt.

We learned God was preparing Joseph for a big job even when Joseph was not aware of it. We were excited to see that God never left Joseph, even through all of the trials he experienced.